MW00763275

for

Becki

with

blessings from

Victoria, Robin & Family

*Praise the LORD. Give thanks
to the LORD, for he is good;
his love endures forever.*

—Psalm 106:1 (NIV)

Authentic Publishing
We welcome your questions and comments.

USA	1820 Jet Stream Drive, Colorado Springs, CO 80921
	www.authenticbooks.com
UK	9 Holdom Avenue, Bletchley, Milton Keynes, Bucks, MK1
	1QR
	www.authenticmedia.co.uk
India	Logos Bhavan, Medchal Road, Jeedimetla Village,
	Secunderabad
	500 055, A.P.

God's Promises on Praise and Worship
ISBN 978-1-934068-89-2

Copyright © 2008 by The Livingstone Corporation

Livingstone project staff includes Andy Culbertson, Linda Taylor, Joan
Guest, Everett O'Bryan. Interior design by Lindsay Galvin and Larry
Taylor.

Published in 2008 by Authentic.
A catalog record for this book is available from the Library of Congress.

13 12 11 10 09 08 / 1 2 3 4 5 6

Printed in the United States of America

GOD'S PROMISES

on Praise and Worship

CONTENTS

A BLUEPRINT FOR

Worship

*Every living thing, praise
the Lord! Praise the Lord!*

—Psalm 150:6 (ERV)

The Participants in
PRAISE AND WORSHIP

Bless the LORD, all His works, in all
places of His dominion. Bless the LORD,
O my soul!
—*Psalm 103:22 (NKJV)*

The heavens declare the glory of God;
the skies proclaim the work of his
hands.
—*Psalm 19:1 (NIV)*

Then I heard every living thing that
is in heaven and on earth and under
the earth and in the sea. I heard every
thing in all these places. I heard them
all saying: "All praise and honor and
glory and power forever and ever to the
One that sits on the throne and to the
Lamb!"
—*Revelation 5:13 (ERV)*

Everything on earth, praise the Lord!
Great sea animals in the oceans, praise
the Lord! God made the fire and hail,
the snow and smoke, and all the stormy
winds. God made the mountains and
hills, the fruit trees and cedar trees.
God made all the wild animals and
cattle, the reptiles and birds. God made
the kings and nations on earth. God
made the leaders and judges. God made
the young men and women. God made
the old and young people. Praise the
Lord's name! Honor his name forever!
Everything in heaven and earth, praise
him!

—*Psalm 148:7–13 (ERV)*

I will give You thanks in the great
assembly; I will praise You among many
people.

—*Psalm 35:18 (NKJV)*

Be happy, heavens! Rejoice, earth! Sea
and everything in it, shout with joy!
Fields and everything growing on them,
be happy! Trees in the forest, sing and
be happy! Be happy because the Lord
is coming. The Lord is coming to rule
the world. He will rule the world with
justice and fairness.

—*Psalm 96:11–13 (ERV)*

Sing for joy, O heavens! Rejoice, O
earth! Burst into song, O mountains!
For the LORD has comforted his people
and will have compassion on them in
their sorrow.

—*Isaiah 49:13 (NLT)*

Sing a new song to the LORD! Sing his
praises from the ends of the earth!
Sing, all you who sail the seas, all you
who live in distant coastlands.

—*Isaiah 42:10 (NLT)*

The LORD is good to everyone. He showers compassion on all his creation. All of your works will thank you, LORD, and your faithful followers will praise you.

      —Psalm 145:9–10 (NLT)

Shout for joy to the LORD, all the earth, burst into jubilant song with music.

      —Psalm 98:4 (NIV)

Sing, O heavens, for the LORD has done it! Shout, you lower parts of the earth; break forth into singing, you mountains, O forest, and every tree in it! For the LORD has redeemed Jacob, and glorified Himself in Israel.

      —Isaiah 44:23 (NKJV)

Praise the LORD. Sing to the LORD a new song, his praise in the assembly of the saints.

      —Psalm 149:1 (NIV)

The people who blew the trumpets and the people who sang were like one person. They made one sound when they praised and thanked the Lord. They made a loud noise with the trumpets, cymbals, and instruments of music. They sang the song, Praise the Lord Because He is Good. His True Love Continues Forever. Then the Lord's temple was filled with a cloud.
    —*2 Chronicles 5:13 (ERV)*

The next day the great crowd that had come for the Feast heard that Jesus was on his way to Jerusalem. They took palm branches and went out to meet him, shouting,

"Hosanna!"

"Blessed is he who comes in the name of the Lord!"

"Blessed is the King of Israel!
    —*John 12:12–13 (NIV)*

Then David said to the whole assembly, "Give praise to the LORD your God!" And the entire assembly praised the LORD, the God of their ancestors, and they bowed low and knelt before the LORD and the king.

—*1 Chronicles 29:20 (NLT)*

Stand up and bless the LORD your God forever and ever! Blessed be Your glorious name, which is exalted above all blessing and praise! You alone are the LORD; You have made heaven, the heaven of heavens, with all their host, the earth and everything on it, the seas and all that is in them, and You preserve them all. The host of heaven worships You.

—*Nehemiah 9:5–6 (NKJV)*

I bless the Lord all the time. His praise is always on my lips.
>—*Psalm 34:1 (ERV)*

This is the day the LORD has made; We will rejoice and be glad in it.
>—*Psalm 118:24 (NKJV)*

People were amazed when they saw that people that could not speak were able to speak again. Crippled people were made strong again. People that could not walk were able to walk again. The blind were able to see again. All the people thanked the God of Israel (the Jews) for this.
>—*Matthew 15:31 (ERV)*

When you have eaten and are satisfied, praise the LORD your God for the good land he has given you.
—*Deuteronomy 8:10 (NIV)*

Praise the LORD! I will thank the LORD with all my heart as I meet with his godly people.
—*Psalm 111:1 (NLT)*

When I am afraid, I put my trust in you. I trust God, so I am not afraid of what people can do to me! I praise God for his promise to me.
—*Psalm 56:3–4 (ERV)*

Sing to the LORD, praise his name; proclaim his salvation day after day.
—*Psalm 96:2 (NIV)*

Every day I will bless You, and I will praise Your name forever and ever.
—*Psalm 145:2 (NKJV)*

The Tools for

Praise the LORD. Praise God in his sanctuary; praise him in his mighty heavens. Praise him for his acts of power; praise him for his surpassing greatness. Praise him with the sounding of the trumpet, praise him with the harp and lyre, praise him with tambourine and dancing, praise him with the strings and flute, praise him with the clash of cymbals, praise him with resounding cymbals. Let everything that has breath praise the LORD. Praise the LORD.
—*Psalm 150:1–6 (NIV)*

Lord, you make us truly happy with the things you did. We gladly sing about those things.
—*Psalm 92:4 (ERV)*

Who may ascend the hill of the LORD? Who may stand in his holy place? He who has clean hands and a pure heart, who does not lift up his soul to an idol or swear by what is false.

> —*Psalm 24:3–4 (NIV)*

But the time is coming—indeed it's here now—when true worshipers will worship the Father in spirit and in truth. The Father is looking for those who will worship him that way. For God is Spirit, so those who worship him must worship in spirit and in truth.

> —*John 4:23–24 (NLT)*

Come, let us praise the Lord! Let's shout praises to the Rock, who saves us. Let's sing songs of thanks to the Lord. Let's sing happy songs of praise to him.

> —*Psalm 95:1–2 (ERV)*

Sing to the LORD, all the earth; proclaim the good news of His salvation from day to day. Declare His glory among the nations, His wonders among all peoples.

  —1 Chronicles 16:23–24 (NKJV)

Let the godly sing for joy to the LORD; it is fitting for the pure to praise him.

  —Psalm 33:1 (NLT)

Be filled with the Holy Spirit, singing psalms and hymns and spiritual songs among yourselves, and making music to the Lord in your hearts. And give thanks for everything to God the Father in the name of our Lord Jesus Christ.

  —Ephesians 5:18–20 (NLT)

My soul shall be satisfied as with marrow and fatness, and my mouth shall praise You with joyful lips.

  —Psalm 63:5 (NKJV)

At the dedication of the wall of Jerusalem, the Levites were sought out from where they lived and were brought to Jerusalem to celebrate joyfully the dedication with songs of thanksgiving and with the music of cymbals, harps and lyres.

—*Nehemiah 12:27 (NIV)*

And I will play the harp and praise you. My God, I will sing that you can be trusted. I will play songs on my lyre for the Holy One of Israel.

—*Psalm 71:22 (ERV)*

Therefore I will give thanks to You, O LORD, among the Gentiles, and sing praises to Your name.

—*2 Samuel 22:50 (NKJV)*

O God, my heart is steadfast; I will sing and give praise, even with my glory.

—*Psalm 108:1 (NKJV)*

Sing for joy to God our strength; shout aloud to the God of Jacob! Begin the music, strike the tambourine, play the melodious harp and lyre.

—*Psalm 81:1–2 (NIV)*

It is good to give thanks to the LORD, and to sing praises to Your name, O Most High; to declare Your lovingkindness in the morning, and Your faithfulness every night, on an instrument of ten strings, on the lute, and on the harp, with harmonious sound.

—*Psalm 92:1–3 (NKJV)*

Sing out your thanks to the LORD; sing praises to our God with a harp.

—*Psalm 147:7 (NLT)*

Lift up your hands in the sanctuary, and bless the LORD.

—*Psalm 134:2 (NKJV)*

Harps and lyres, let's wake up the sun! Lord, we will praise you among the nations. We will praise you among other people.

—*Psalm 108:2–3 (ERV)*

Praise his name with dancing, accompanied by tambourine and harp. For the LORD delights in his people; he crowns the humble with victory.

—*Psalm 149:3–4 (NLT)*

So I say: "The Lord saved me. So we will sing and play songs in the Lord's temple all our lives."

—*Isaiah 38:20 (ERV)*

Your love is better than life. My lips praise you. Yes, I will praise you in my life. In your name, I lift my arms in prayer.

—*Psalm 63:3–4 (ERV)*

I lift up my hands to your commands, which I love, and I meditate on your decrees.

> —*Psalm 119:48 (NIV)*

Praise the LORD with the harp; make music to him on the ten-stringed lyre. Sing to him a new song; play skillfully, and shout for joy. For the word of the LORD is right and true; he is faithful in all he does.

> —*Psalm 33:2–4 (NIV)*

Let us search out and examine our ways, and turn back to the LORD; let us lift our hearts and hands to God in heaven.

> —*Lamentations 3:40–41 (NKJV)*

Shout for joy to the LORD, all the earth. Worship the LORD with gladness; come before him with joyful songs.

> —*Psalm 100:1–2 (NIV)*

The Focus for

Jesus replied, "The Scriptures say, 'You must worship the Lord your God and serve only him.'"

      —Luke 4:8 (NLT)

For I desire mercy and not sacrifice, and the knowledge of God more than burnt offerings.

      —Hosea 6:6 (NKJV)

You must fear the LORD your God and worship him and cling to him. Your oaths must be in his name alone. He alone is your God, the only one who is worthy of your praise, the one who has done these mighty miracles that you have seen with your own eyes.

      —Deuteronomy 10:20–21 (NLT)

He takes no pleasure in the strength of a horse or in human might. No, the LORD's delight is in those who fear him, those who put their hope in his unfailing love. Glorify the LORD, O Jerusalem! Praise your God, O Zion!

—*Psalm 147:10–12 (NLT)*

And the statutes, the ordinances, the law, and the commandment which He wrote for you, you shall be careful to observe forever; you shall not fear other gods. And the covenant that I have made with you, you shall not forget, nor shall you fear other gods. But the LORD your God you shall fear; and He will deliver you from the hand of all your enemies.

—*2 Kings 17:37–39 (NKJV)*

Then they will know that you are God.
They will know your name is YAHWEH.
They will know that you, God Most-
High, are the God of the whole world!
　　　—*Psalm 83:18 (ERV)*

Since we are receiving a Kingdom that
is unshakable, let us be thankful and
please God by worshiping him with holy
fear and awe.
　　　—*Hebrews 12:28 (NLT)*

Observe my Sabbaths and have
reverence for my sanctuary. I am the
LORD.
　　　—*Leviticus 26:2 (NIV)*

Every person on earth should fear and
respect the Lord. All the people in the
world should fear him.
　　　—*Psalm 33:8 (ERV)*

Worship

GOD FOR WHO HE IS

The four living creatures, each having six wings, were full of eyes around and within. And they do not rest day or night, saying: "Holy, holy, holy, Lord God Almighty, Who was and is and is to come!"

—Revelation 4:8 (NKJV)

od's Promises God's Promises God's

Ever LOVING

Dear friends, we should love each other, because love comes from God. The person who loves has become God's child. And so the person who loves knows God.
> —*1 John 4:7 (ERV)*

I hate people who worship false gods. I trust only in the Lord. God, your kindness makes me very happy. You have seen my suffering. You know about the troubles I have.
> —*Psalm 31:6–7 (ERV)*

Live a life filled with love, following the example of Christ. He loved us and offered himself as a sacrifice for us, a pleasing aroma to God.
> —*Ephesians 5:2 (NLT)*

In this the love of God was manifested toward us, that God has sent His only begotten Son into the world, that we might live through Him. In this is love, not that we loved God, but that He loved us and sent His Son to be the propitiation for our sins.

—*1 John 4:9–10 (NKJV)*

You are forgiving and good, O Lord, abounding in love to all who call to you.

—*Psalm 86:5 (NIV)*

Your unfailing love, O LORD, is as vast as the heavens; your faithfulness reaches beyond the clouds. . . . How precious is your unfailing love, O God! All humanity finds shelter in the shadow of your wings.

—*Psalm 36:5, 7 (NLT)*

And I pray that you, being rooted and established in love, may have power, together with all the saints, to grasp how wide and long and high and deep is the love of Christ.
>—*Ephesians 3:17–18 (NIV)*

My Master, I praise you to everyone. I sing songs of praise about you to every nation. Your true love is higher than the highest clouds in the sky!
>—*Psalm 57:9–10 (ERV)*

He loves righteousness and justice; the earth is full of the goodness of the LORD.
>—*Psalm 33:5 (NKJV)*

Praise God! God did not turn away from me—he listened to my prayer. God showed his love to me!
>—*Psalm 66:20 (ERV)*

All WISE

With Him are wisdom and strength, He has counsel and understanding.
—*Job 12:13 (NKJV)*

"My thoughts are nothing like your thoughts," says the LORD. "And my ways are far beyond anything you could imagine. For just as the heavens are higher than the earth, so my ways are higher than your ways and my thoughts higher than your thoughts."
—*Isaiah 55:8–9 (NLT)*

Oh, the depth of the riches both of the wisdom and knowledge of God! How unsearchable are His judgments and His ways past finding out!
—*Romans 11:33 (NKJV)*

For the LORD gives wisdom, and
from his mouth come knowledge and
understanding.
        —*Proverbs 2:6 (NIV)*

Yes, I know what you say is true. But
how can a man win an argument with
God? A person can't argue with God!
God could ask 1,000 questions and no
person could answer even one! God is
very wise and his power is very great.
No person can fight God and not be
hurt.
        —*Job 9:2–4 (ERV)*

Then the secret was revealed to Daniel
in a night vision. So Daniel blessed
the God of heaven. Daniel answered
and said: "Blessed be the name of God
forever and ever, for wisdom and might
are His."
        —*Daniel 2:19–20 (NKJV)*

Where is the wise man? Where is the scholar? Where is the philosopher of this age? Has not God made foolish the wisdom of the world? For since in the wisdom of God the world through its wisdom did not know him, God was pleased through the foolishness of what was preached to save those who believe. . . . For the foolishness of God is wiser than man's wisdom, and the weakness of God is stronger than man's strength.

—*1 Corinthians 1:20–21, 25 (NIV)*

God is the One who used his power and made the earth. God used his wisdom and built the world. With his understanding, God stretched out the sky over the earth.

—*Jeremiah 10:12 (ERV)*

From where then does wisdom come? And where is the place of understanding? It is hidden from the eyes of all living, and concealed from the birds of the air. . . . God understands its way, and He knows its place.

—*Job 28:20–21, 23 (NKJV)*

O LORD, what a variety of things you have made! In wisdom you have made them all. The earth is full of your creatures.

—*Psalm 104:24 (NLT)*

Always FAITHFUL

Understand, therefore, that the LORD your God is indeed God. He is the faithful God who keeps his covenant for a thousand generations and lavishes his unfailing love on those who love him and obey his commands.

—*Deuteronomy 7:9 (NLT)*

Praise God as I speak the Lord's name! The Rock (the Lord)—his work is perfect! Why? Because all his ways are right! God is true and faithful. He is good and honest.

—*Deuteronomy 32:3–4 (ERV)*

The faithful love of the LORD never ends! His mercies never cease. Great is his faithfulness; his mercies begin afresh each morning.

—*Lamentations 3:22–23 (NLT)*

No temptation has seized you except what is common to man. And God is faithful; he will not let you be tempted beyond what you can bear. But when you are tempted, he will also provide a way out so that you can stand up under it.

—*1 Corinthians 10:13 (NIV)*

I will praise you, O Lord, among the nations; I will sing of you among the peoples. For great is your love, reaching to the heavens; your faithfulness reaches to the skies.

—*Psalm 57:9–10 (NIV)*

For your kingdom is an everlasting kingdom. You rule throughout all generations. The LORD always keeps his promises; he is gracious in all he does.

—*Psalm 145:13 (NLT)*

He causes us to remember his wonderful works. How gracious and merciful is our LORD! . . . All he does is just and good, and all his commandments are trustworthy. They are forever true, to be obeyed faithfully and with integrity.

—*Psalm 111:4, 7–8 (NLT)*

O LORD, You are my God. I will exalt You, I will praise Your name, for You have done wonderful things; Your counsels of old are faithfulness and truth.

—*Isaiah 25:1 (NKJV)*

But the Lord is faithful. He will give you strength and protect you from the Evil One (the devil).

—*2 Thessalonians 3:3 (ERV)*

God, who has called you into fellowship
with his Son Jesus Christ our Lord, is
faithful.

—*1 Corinthians 1:9 (NIV)*

But you, O Lord, are a God of
compassion and mercy, slow to get
angry and filled with unfailing love and
faithfulness.

—*Psalm 86:15 (NLT)*

He who calls you is faithful, who also
will do it.

—*1 Thessalonians 5:24 (NKJV)*

Strong AND POWERFUL

The LORD is my strength and song, and
He has become my salvation; He is my
God, and I will praise Him; My father's
God, and I will exalt Him.
> —*Exodus 15:2 (NKJV)*

He said, "Lord my strength, I love you!
The Lord is my Rock, my Fortress, my
Place of Safety." My God is my Rock.
I run to him for protection. God is my
shield. His power saves me. The Lord is
my hiding place high in the hills.
> —*Psalm 18:1–2 (ERV)*

Proclaim the power of God, whose
majesty is over Israel, whose power is in
the skies.
> —*Psalm 68:34 (NIV)*

But with your kindness you lead the people you saved. And with your strength you lead them to your holy and pleasant land.

—*Exodus 15:13 (ERV)*

For who is God, except the LORD? And who is a rock, except our God? God is my strength and power, and He makes my way perfect.

—*2 Samuel 22:32–33 (NKJV)*

God is our storehouse of strength. In him, we can always find help in times of trouble.

—*Psalm 46:1 (ERV)*

After these things I heard a loud voice of a great multitude in heaven, saying, "Alleluia! Salvation and glory and honor and power belong to the Lord our God!"

—*Revelation 19:1 (NKJV)*

Surely God is my salvation; I will trust and not be afraid. The LORD, the LORD, is my strength and my song; he has become my salvation.

—*Isaiah 12:2 (NIV)*

To You, O my Strength, I will sing praises; for God is my defense, my God of mercy.

—*Psalm 59:17 (NKJV)*

One thing God has spoken, two things have I heard: that you, O God, are strong, and that you, O Lord, are loving. Surely you will reward each person according to what he has done.

—*Psalm 62:11–12 (NIV)*

The LORD gives his people strength. He is a safe fortress for his anointed king.

—*Psalm 28:8 (NLT)*

God, get up and scatter your enemies. May all of his enemies run from him. May your enemies be scattered, like smoke blown away by the wind. May your enemies be destroyed, like wax melting in a fire. But good people are happy. Good people have a happy time together with God. Good people enjoy themselves and are very happy! Sing to God. Sing praises to his name. Prepare the way for God. He rides his chariot over the desert. His name is YAH. Praise his name! In his holy temple, God is like a father to orphans. God takes care of widows. God gives lonely people a home. God takes his people out of prison. They are very happy. But people who turn against God, will stay in their hot prison. . . .

God, the God of Israel, came to Mount Sinai, and the sky melted. God, you sent the rain to make a tired, old land strong again. Your animals came back to that land. God, you gave many good things to the poor people there. . . .

Kings on earth, sing to God! Sing songs of praise to our Master! Sing to God! He rides his chariot through the ancient skies. Listen to his powerful voice! God is more powerful than any of your gods. The God of Israel makes his people strong. God is wonderful in his temple. The God of Israel gives strength and power to his people. Praise God!

—*Psalm 68:1–6, 8–10,32–35 (ERV)*

 *Great* AND AWESOME

How awesome is the LORD Most High,
the great King over all the earth!
>—*Psalm 47:2 (NIV)*

Praise the LORD! Praise God in his
sanctuary; praise him in his mighty
heaven! Praise him for his mighty
works; praise his unequaled greatness!
>—*Psalm 150:1–2 (NLT)*

God is powerful and dreadful. He
enforces peace in the heavens.
>—*Job 25:2 (NLT)*

For the LORD your God is God of gods
and Lord of lords, the great God, mighty
and awesome, who shows no partiality
nor takes a bribe.
>—*Deuteronomy 10:17 (NKJV)*

Oh, sing to the LORD a new song!
Sing to the LORD, all the earth. Sing
to the LORD, bless His name; proclaim
the good news of His salvation from
day to day. Declare His glory among
the nations, His wonders among all
peoples.

For the LORD is great and greatly to
be praised; He is to be feared above all
gods. For all the gods of the peoples
are idols, but the LORD made the
heavens. Honor and majesty are before
Him; strength and beauty are in His
sanctuary. Give to the LORD, O families
of the peoples, give to the LORD glory
and strength. Give to the LORD the glory
due His name; bring an offering, and
come into His courts. Oh, worship the
LORD in the beauty of holiness! Tremble
before Him, all the earth.

—Psalm 96:1–9 (NKJV)

No, do not be afraid of those nations, for the LORD your God is among you, and he is a great and awesome God.
> —*Deuteronomy 7:21 (NLT)*

Lord, there is no one like you! You are great! Your name is great and powerful!
> —*Jeremiah 10:6 (ERV)*

And God is like that too! God's golden glory shines from the Holy Mountain. There is a bright light around God. God All-Powerful is great! We can't understand God! God is very powerful, but he is also good and fair to us. God doesn't want to hurt us!
> —*Job 37:22–23 (ERV)*

Who among the gods is like you, O LORD? Who is like you—majestic in holiness, awesome in glory, working wonders?
> —*Exodus 15:11 (NIV)*

Great is the LORD! He is most worthy
of praise! No one can measure his
greatness.
—*Psalm 145:3 (NLT)*

Yours, O LORD, is the greatness, the
power and the glory, the victory and the
majesty; for all that is in heaven and in
earth is Yours; Yours is the kingdom, O
LORD, and You are exalted as head over
all.
—*1 Chronicles 29:11 (NKJV)*

God, you are great! You do amazing
things! You, and you only, are God!
—*Psalm 86:10 (ERV)*

O LORD, God of heaven, the great and awesome God, who keeps his covenant of love with those who love him and obey his commands, let your ear be attentive and your eyes open to hear the prayer your servant is praying before you day and night for your servants, the people of Israel. I confess the sins we Israelites, including myself and my father's house, have committed against you.

—Nehemiah 1:5–6 (NIV)

Merciful AND GRACIOUS

For He who is mighty has done great things for me, and holy is His name. And His mercy is on those who fear Him From generation to generation.
—*Luke 1:49–50 (NKJV)*

But when the kindness and love of God our Savior appeared, he saved us, not because of righteous things we had done, but because of his mercy. He saved us through the washing of rebirth and renewal by the Holy Spirit.
—*Titus 3:4–5 (NIV)*

LORD, I have heard of your fame; I stand in awe of your deeds, O LORD. Renew them in our day, in our time make them known; in wrath remember mercy.
—*Habakkuk 3:2 (NIV)*

Blessed be the God and Father of our Lord Jesus Christ, who according to His abundant mercy has begotten us again to a living hope through the resurrection of Jesus Christ from the dead.

—*1 Peter 1:3 (NKJV)*

For everyone has sinned; we all fall short of God's glorious standard. Yet God, with undeserved kindness, declares that we are righteous. He did this through Christ Jesus when he freed us from the penalty for our sins.

—*Romans 3:23–24 (NLT)*

Praise the Lord! He heard my prayer for mercy. The Lord is my strength. He is my shield. I trusted him. And he helped me. I am very happy! And I sing songs of praise to him.

—*Psalm 28:6–7 (ERV)*

But God's mercy is very great, and
God loved us very much. We were
spiritually dead. We were dead because
of the things we did wrong against God.
But God gave us new life with Christ.
You have been saved by God's grace
(kindness).

—*Ephesians 2:4–5 (ERV)*

 AND JUST

Oh, thank the Lord—he is good. The Lord's love continues forever.

—*1 Chronicles 16:34 (ERV)*

I praise the Lord with all my heart. Lord, I will tell about all the wonderful things you did. You make me so very happy. God Most-High, I praise your name. . . . You are the good judge. You sat on your throne as judge. Lord, you listened to my case. And you made the decision about me.

—*Psalm 9:1–2, 4 (ERV)*

I will thank the LORD because he is just; I will sing praise to the name of the LORD Most High.

—*Psalm 7:17 (NLT)*

Therefore the LORD will wait, that He may be gracious to you; and therefore He will be exalted, that He may have mercy on you. For the LORD is a God of justice; blessed are all those who wait for Him.

—*Isaiah 30:18 (NKJV)*

The Lord All-Powerful will judge fairly, and people will know he is great. The Holy God will do the things that are right, and the people will respect him.

—*Isaiah 5:16 (ERV)*

And will not God bring about justice for his chosen ones, who cry out to him day and night? Will he keep putting them off? I tell you, he will see that they get justice, and quickly. However, when the Son of Man comes, will he find faith on the earth?

—*Luke 18:7–8 (NIV)*

For the LORD is righteous, he loves
justice; upright men will see his face.
—*Psalm 11:7 (NIV)*

There is no one holy like the LORD;
there is no one besides you; there is no
Rock like our God.
—*1 Samuel 2:2 (NIV)*

Listen to Me, My people; and give
ear to Me, O My nation: For law will
proceed from Me, and I will make My
justice rest as a light of the peoples. My
righteousness is near, My salvation has
gone forth, and My arms will judge the
peoples; the coastlands will wait upon
Me, and on My arm they will trust.
—*Isaiah 51:4–5 (NKJV)*

Sing to the LORD! Praise the LORD!
For though I was poor and needy, he
rescued me from my oppressors.
—*Jeremiah 20:13 (NLT)*

Lord, you heard what poor people want. Listen to their prayers and do what they ask! Lord, protect the children without parents. Don't let sad people suffer more troubles. Make bad people too afraid to stay here.

—*Psalm 10:17–18 (ERV)*

Who will not fear you, Lord, and glorify your name? For you alone are holy. All nations will come and worship before you, for your righteous deeds have been revealed.

—*Revelation 15:4 (NLT)*

Praise the Lord and honor his name! Worship him in your special clothes.

—*Psalm 29:2 (ERV)*

I will sing about love and fairness. Lord, I will sing to you.

—*Psalm 101:1 (ERV)*

Let each generation tell its children of your mighty acts; let them proclaim your power. . . . Everyone will share the story of your wonderful goodness; they will sing with joy about your righteousness.

—Psalm 145:4, 7 (NLT)

Let the sea roar, and all its fullness, the world and those who dwell in it; let the rivers clap their hands; let the hills be joyful together before the LORD, for He is coming to judge the earth. With righteousness He shall judge the world, and the peoples with equity.

—Psalm 98:7–9 (NKJV)

Oh, how great is Your goodness, which You have laid up for those who fear You, which You have prepared for those who trust in You in the presence of the sons of men!

—Psalm 31:19 (NKJV)

Glorious SOVEREIGN

Yours, O LORD, is the greatness and the power and the glory and the majesty and the splendor, for everything in heaven and earth is yours. Yours, O LORD, is the kingdom; you are exalted as head over all. Wealth and honor come from you; you are the ruler of all things. In your hands are strength and power to exalt and give strength to all. Now, our God, we give you thanks, and praise your glorious name.

—*1 Chronicles 29:11–13 (NIV)*

The LORD reigns, he is robed in majesty; the LORD is robed in majesty and is armed with strength. The world is firmly established; it cannot be moved. Your throne was established long ago; you are from all eternity.

—*Psalm 93:1–2 (NIV)*

For as the waters fill the sea, the earth will be filled with an awareness of the glory of the LORD.

—*Habakkuk 2:14 (NLT)*

Who is like You, O LORD, among the gods? Who is like You, glorious in holiness, fearful in praises, doing wonders?

—*Exodus 15:11 (NKJV)*

The Lord has glory and honor. The Lord is like a bright, shining light.

—*1 Chronicles 16:27 (ERV)*

May they sing of the ways of the LORD, for the glory of the LORD is great.

—*Psalm 138:5 (NIV)*

I will extol You, my God, O King; and I will bless Your name forever and ever. Every day I will bless You, and I will praise Your name forever and ever.

—*Psalm 145:1–2 (NKJV)*

Forgiving REDEEMER

As for our Redeemer, the LORD of hosts
is His name, the Holy One of Israel.
> —*Isaiah 47:4 (NKJV)*

But as for me, I know that my
Redeemer lives, and he will stand upon
the earth at last.
> —*Job 19:25 (NLT)*

He provided redemption for his people;
he ordained his covenant forever—holy
and awesome is his name.
> —*Psalm 111:9 (NIV)*

This is what the Lord says—Israel's
King and Redeemer, the LORD of
Heaven's Armies: I am the First and the
Last; there is no other God.
> —*Isaiah 44:6 (NLT)*

My soul, praise the Lord! Every part of me, praise his holy name! My soul, praise the Lord! And don't forget that he is truly kind. God forgives us for all the sins we do. He heals all our sicknesses.

—*Psalm 103:1–3 (ERV)*

There is no God like you. You take away people's guilt. God forgives his people that survived. He won't stay angry forever. Why? Because He enjoys being kind. He will come back and comfort us again. He will crush our guilt and throw all of our sins into the deep sea.

—*Micah 7:18–19 (ERV)*

God made us free from the power of darkness (evil). And he brought us into the kingdom of his dear Son (Jesus). The Son paid the price to make us free. In him we have forgiveness of our sins.

—*Colossians 1:13–14 (ERV)*

If you return to the Almighty, you will be restored—so clean up your life. . . . Then you will take delight in the Almighty and look up to God. You will pray to him, and he will hear you, and you will fulfill your vows to him.

—*Job 22:23, 26–27 (NLT)*

If My people who are called by My name will humble themselves, and pray and seek My face, and turn from their wicked ways, then I will hear from heaven, and will forgive their sin and heal their land.

—*2 Chronicles 7:14 (NKJV)*

This is what the LORD says—your Redeemer, who formed you in the womb: I am the LORD, who has made all things, who alone stretched out the heavens, who spread out the earth by myself.

—*Isaiah 44:24 (NIV)*

Give thanks to the LORD, for he is good; his love endures forever. Let the redeemed of the LORD say this—those he redeemed from the hand of the foe.
　　—Psalm 107:1–2 (NIV)

For you know that God paid a ransom to save you from the empty life you inherited from your ancestors. And the ransom he paid was not mere gold or silver. It was the precious blood of Christ, the sinless, spotless Lamb of God. God chose him as your ransom long before the world began, but he has now revealed him to you in these last days. Through Christ you have come to trust in God. And you have placed your faith and hope in God because he raised Christ from the dead and gave him great glory.
　　—1 Peter 1:18–21 (NLT)

If we confess our sins, he is faithful and just and will forgive us our sins and purify us from all unrighteousness.
—1 John 1:9 (NIV)

He will redeem his soul from going down to the Pit, and his life shall see the light.
—Job 33:28 (NKJV)

He chose us in Him before the foundation of the world, that we should be holy and without blame before Him in love, having predestined us to adoption as sons by Jesus Christ to Himself, according to the good pleasure of His will, to the praise of the glory of His grace, by which He made us accepted in the Beloved. In Him we have redemption through His blood, the forgiveness of sins, according to the riches of His grace.
—Ephesians 1:4–7 (NKJV)

But Christ has rescued us from the curse pronounced by the law. When he was hung on the cross, he took upon himself the curse for our wrongdoing. For it is written in the Scriptures, "Cursed is everyone who is hung on a tree." Through Christ Jesus, God has blessed the Gentiles with the same blessing he promised to Abraham, so that we who are believers might receive the promised Holy Spirit through faith.

—*Galatians 3:13–14 (NLT)*

My lips shall greatly rejoice when I sing to You, and my soul, which You have redeemed.

—*Psalm 71:23 (NKJV)*

Those people would remember that God was their Rock, they would remember that God Most-High saved them.

—*Psalm 78:35 (ERV)*

Israel, trust the Lord. True love is found only with the Lord. The Lord saves us again and again.

—*Psalm 130:7 (ERV)*

Praise the Lord, the God of Israel, because he has visited and redeemed his people.

—*Luke 1:68 (NLT)*

Worship

GOD FOR WHAT HE HAS DONE

*He restores my soul. He guides
me in paths of righteousness for
his name's sake.*

—Psalm 23:3 (NIV)

Answered PRAYER

And in that day you will say: "Praise the LORD, call upon His name; declare His deeds among the peoples, make mention that His name is exalted. Sing to the LORD, for He has done excellent things; this is known in all the earth."
—*Isaiah 12:4–5 (NKJV)*

The LORD has heard my cry for mercy; the LORD accepts my prayer.
—*Psalm 6:9 (NIV)*

Praise the Lord! He promised to give rest to his people, Israel. And he has given us rest! The Lord used his servant Moses and made many good promises to the people of Israel. And the Lord has kept every one of those promises!
—*1 Kings 8:56 (ERV)*

During the night the mystery was revealed to Daniel in a vision. Then Daniel praised the God of heaven . . . "I thank and praise you, O God of my fathers: You have given me wisdom and power, you have made known to me what we asked of you, you have made known to us the dream of the king."
—*Daniel 2:19, 23 (NIV)*

God listened to me. God heard my prayer. Praise God! God did not turn away from me—he listened to my prayer. God showed his love to me!
—*Psalm 66:19–20 (ERV)*

The LORD is my strength and shield. I trust him with all my heart. He helps me, and my heart is filled with joy. I burst out in songs of thanksgiving.
—*Psalm 28:7 (NLT)*

In my distress I called upon the LORD,
and cried out to my God; He heard
my voice from His temple, and my cry
entered His ears.
　　　—*2 Samuel 22:7 (NKJV)*

We cried out to the LORD, the God of
our ancestors. He heard our cries and
saw our hardship, toil, and oppression.
So the LORD brought us out of Egypt
with a strong hand and powerful arm,
with overwhelming terror, and with
miraculous signs and wonders.
　　　—*Deuteronomy 26:7–8 (NLT)*

Blessings

For you bless the godly, O LORD, you surround them with your shield of love.
—*Psalm 5:12 (NLT)*

You have turned for me my mourning into dancing; You have put off my sackcloth and clothed me with gladness, to the end that my glory may sing praise to You and not be silent. O LORD my God, I will give thanks to You forever.
—*Psalm 30:11–12 (NKJV)*

You will teach me the right way to live. Just being with you, Lord, will bring complete happiness. Being at your right side will bring happiness forever.
—*Psalm 16:11 (ERV)*

Praise be to the Lord, to God our
Savior, who daily bears our burdens.
 —*Psalm 68:19 (NIV)*

O LORD my God, I cried out to You, and
You healed me.
 —*Psalm 30:2 (NKJV)*

Sing to the LORD! Praise the LORD! For
He has delivered the life of the poor
from the hand of evildoers.
 —*Jeremiah 20:13 (NKJV)*

I waited patiently for the LORD; and He
inclined to me, and heard my cry. He
also brought me up out of a horrible
pit, out of the miry clay, and set my feet
upon a rock, and established my steps.
He has put a new song in my mouth—
Praise to our God; many will see it and
fear, and will trust in the LORD.
 —*Psalm 40:1–3 (NKJV)*

I love the LORD, because He has heard my voice and my supplications. Because He has inclined His ear to me, therefore I will call upon Him as long as I live. The pains of death surrounded me, and the pangs of Sheol laid hold of me; I found trouble and sorrow. Then I called upon the name of the LORD: "O LORD, I implore You, deliver my soul!" Gracious is the LORD, and righteous; yes, our God is merciful. The LORD preserves the simple; I was brought low, and He saved me. Return to your rest, O my soul, for the LORD has dealt bountifully with you.

—Psalm 116:1–7 (NKJV)

You have endowed him with eternal blessings and given him the joy of your presence.

—Psalm 21:6 (NLT)

But I trust in your unfailing love. I will rejoice because you have rescued me. I will sing to the LORD because he is good to me.

—*Psalm 13:5–6 (NLT)*

Lord my Master, you are God. And I can trust the things you say. And you said that these good things will happen to me, your servant. Now, please, bless my family. Let them stand before you and serve you forever. Lord my Master, you yourself said these things. You yourself blessed my family with a blessing that will continue forever.

—*2 Samuel 7:28–29 (ERV)*

The LORD remembers us and will bless us: He will bless the house of Israel, he will bless the house of Aaron, he will bless those who fear the LORD—small and great alike.

—*Psalm 115:12–13 (NIV)*

There, in the presence of the LORD your
God, you and your families shall eat and
shall rejoice in everything you have put
your hand to, because the LORD your God
has blessed you.

—*Deuteronomy 12:7 (NIV)*

Israel, you are blessed. No other nation
is like you. The Lord saved you. The Lord
is like a strong shield protecting you.
The Lord is like a powerful sword. Your
enemies will be afraid of you. And you will
trample their holy places!

—*Deuteronomy 33:29 (ERV)*

I bless the Lord all the time. His praise is
always on my lips. Humble people, listen
and be happy while I brag about the Lord.
Praise God with me! Let's honor his name.
I went to God for help. And he listened. He
saved me from all the things I fear.

—*Psalm 34:1–4 (ERV)*

Praise the LORD, O my soul, and forget not all his benefits—who forgives all your sins and heals all your diseases, who redeems your life from the pit and crowns you with love and compassion, who satisfies your desires with good things so that your youth is renewed like the eagle's.

—Psalm 103:2–5 (NIV)

They were in trouble, so they called to the Lord for help. And he saved them from their troubles. God gave the command and healed them. So those people were saved from the grave. Thank the Lord for his love and for the amazing things he does for people.

—Psalm 107:19–21 (ERV)

He heals the brokenhearted and binds up their wounds.

—Psalm 147:3 (NIV)

Comfort AND CONSOLATION

I will comfort you there in Jerusalem as a mother comforts her child.
—*Isaiah 66:13 (NLT)*

The Lord will save his people. They will return to Zion with joy. They will be very, very happy. Their happiness will be like a crown on their heads forever. They will be singing with joy. All sadness will be gone far away. The Lord says, "I am the One who comforts you. So why should you be afraid of people? They are only people that live and die. They are only humans—they die the same as grass."
—*Isaiah 51:11–12 (ERV)*

Cast all your anxiety on him because he cares for you.
—*1 Peter 5:7 (NIV)*

If I say, "My foot slips," Your mercy, O LORD, will hold me up. In the multitude of my anxieties within me, Your comforts delight my soul.
—*Psalm 94:18–19 (NKJV)*

Come to Me, all you who labor and are heavy laden, and I will give you rest.
—*Matthew 11:28 (NKJV)*

Praise be to the God and Father of our Lord Jesus Christ, the Father of compassion and the God of all comfort, who comforts us in all our troubles, so that we can comfort those in any trouble with the comfort we ourselves have received from God. For just as the sufferings of Christ flow over into our lives, so also through Christ our comfort overflows.
—*2 Corinthians 1:3–5 (NIV)*

A person might be sad when he plants the seeds, but he will be happy when he gathers the crops!

—*Psalm 126:5 (ERV)*

May your unfailing love be my comfort, according to your promise to your servant.

—*Psalm 119:76 (NIV)*

No, I will not abandon you as orphans—I will come to you.

—*John 14:18 (NLT)*

The righteous cry out, and the LORD hears them; he delivers them from all their troubles. The LORD is close to the brokenhearted and saves those who are crushed in spirit.

—*Psalm 34:17–18 (NIV)*

Don't worry, I am with you. Don't be afraid, I am your God. I will make you strong. I will help you. I will support you with my good right hand.

—*Isaiah 41:10 (ERV)*

So be strong and courageous! Do not be afraid and do not panic before them. For the LORD your God will personally go ahead of you. He will neither fail you nor abandon you.

—*Deuteronomy 31:6 (NLT)*

Then shall the virgin rejoice in the dance, and the young men and the old, together; for I will turn their mourning to joy, will comfort them, and make them rejoice rather than sorrow.

—*Jeremiah 31:13 (NKJV)*

The LORD is gracious and righteous; our God is full of compassion.

—*Psalm 116:5 (NIV)*

The LORD rescues the godly; he is their fortress in times of trouble.
—*Psalm 37:39 (NLT)*

Yea, though I walk through the valley of the shadow of death, I will fear no evil; for You are with me; Your rod and Your staff, they comfort me.
—*Psalm 23:4 (NKJV)*

Creation

Then the leaders of the Levites . . .
called out to the people: "Stand up and
praise the LORD your God, for he lives
from everlasting to everlasting!" Then
they prayed: "May your glorious name
be praised! May it be exalted above
all blessing and praise! You alone are
the LORD. You made the skies and the
heavens and all the stars. You made
the earth and the seas and everything
in them. You preserve them all, and the
angels of heaven worship you."
   —*Nehemiah 9:5–6 (NLT)*

The Lord is good to every person. God
shows his mercy to everything he made.
Lord, the things you do bring praise to
you. Your followers bless you.
   —*Psalm 145:9–10 (ERV)*

Praise him, sun and moon! Praise him, all you twinkling stars! Praise him, skies above! Praise him, vapors high above the clouds! Let every created thing give praise to the LORD, for he issued his command, and they came into being. He set them in place forever and ever. His decree will never be revoked. Praise the LORD from the earth, you creatures of the ocean depths, fire and hail, snow and clouds, wind and weather that obey him, mountains and all hills, fruit trees and all cedars, wild animals and all livestock, small scurrying animals and birds.

—*Psalm 148:3–10 (NLT)*

But when you send out your Spirit, Lord, they become healthy! And you make the land like new again!

—*Psalm 104:30 (ERV)*

He alone spreads out the heavens,
And treads on the waves of the sea; He
made the Bear, Orion, and the Pleiades,
And the chambers of the south; He
does great things past finding out, yes,
wonders without number.

—*Job 9:8–10 (NKJV)*

Tremble before him, all the earth! The
world is firmly established; it cannot
be moved. Let the heavens rejoice, let
the earth be glad; let them say among
the nations, "The LORD reigns!" Let the
sea resound, and all that is in it; let
the fields be jubilant, and everything in
them! Then the trees of the forest will
sing, they will sing for joy before the
LORD, for he comes to judge the earth.
Give thanks to the LORD, for he is good;
his love endures forever.

—*1 Chronicles 16:30–34 (NIV)*

Bless the LORD, O my soul! O LORD my God, You are very great: You are clothed with honor and majesty, Who cover Yourself with light as with a garment, Who stretch out the heavens like a curtain. He lays the beams of His upper chambers in the waters, Who makes the clouds His chariot, Who walks on the wings of the wind, Who makes His angels spirits, His ministers a flame of fire.

—*Psalm 104:1–4 (NKJV)*

When I look at the night sky and see the work of your fingers—the moon and the stars you set in place—what are people that you should think about them, mere mortals that you should care for them? Yet you made them only a little lower than God and crowned them with glory and honor.

—*Psalm 8:3–5 (NLT)*

How many are your works, O LORD! In wisdom you made them all; the earth is full of your creatures. There is the sea, vast and spacious, teeming with creatures beyond number—living things both large and small.

—*Psalm 104:24–25 (NIV)*

Guidance

Your Spirit is in every place I go. Lord,
I can't escape you. Lord, if I go east
where the sun rises, you are there. If I
go west to the sea, you are there. Even
there your right hand holds me, and
you lead me by the hand.
>—Psalm 139:7, 9–10 (ERV)

Good and upright is the LORD; therefore
He teaches sinners in the way. The
humble He guides in justice, and the
humble He teaches His way.
>—Psalm 25:8–9 (NKJV)

May people praise you, God! May all
people praise you. May all nations
rejoice and be happy! Why? Because
you judge people fairly. And you rule
over every nation.
>—Psalm 67:3–4 (ERV)

For this is God, our God forever and ever; He will be our guide even to death.
  —*Psalm 48:14 (NKJV)*

Trust in the LORD with all your heart; do not depend on your own understanding. Seek his will in all you do, and he will show you which path to take.
  —*Proverbs 3:5–6 (NLT)*

Peace

Now, brothers and sisters, I say good-
bye. Try to be perfect. Do the things
I have asked you to do. Agree in your
minds with each other, and live in
peace. Then the God of love and peace
will be with you.
—*2 Corinthians 13:11 (ERV)*

I am leaving you with a gift—peace of
mind and heart. And the peace I give is
a gift the world cannot give. So don't be
troubled or afraid.
—*John 14:27 (NLT)*

Therefore, since we have been justified
through faith, we have peace with God
through our Lord Jesus Christ.
—*Romans 5:1 (NIV)*

I go to bed and sleep in peace. Why?
Because, Lord, you lay me down to
sleep in safety.

  —Psalm 4:8 (ERV)

But the wisdom that comes from
heaven is first of all pure; then peace-
loving, considerate, submissive, full
of mercy and good fruit, impartial and
sincere. Peacemakers who sow in peace
raise a harvest of righteousness.

  —James 3:17–18 (NIV)

Nevertheless, the time will come when
I will heal Jerusalem's wounds and give
it prosperity and true peace.

  —Jeremiah 33:6 (NLT)

This message is from the Lord. "I have
good plans for you. I don't plan to hurt
you. I plan to give you hope and a good
future."

  —Jeremiah 29:11 (ERV)

For the kingdom of God is not a matter of eating and drinking, but of righteousness, peace and joy in the Holy Spirit.
>—*Romans 14:17 (NIV)*

I listen carefully to what God the LORD is saying, for he speaks peace to his faithful people. But let them not return to their foolish ways.
>—*Psalm 85:8 (NLT)*

He makes peace in your borders, and fills you with the finest wheat.
>—*Psalm 147:14 (NKJV)*

For a child is born to us, a son is given to us. The government will rest on his shoulders. And he will be called: Wonderful Counselor, Mighty God, Everlasting Father, Prince of Peace.
>—*Isaiah 9:6 (NLT)*

I have told you these things, so that in me you may have peace. In this world you will have trouble. But take heart! I have overcome the world.

     —John 16:33 (NIV)

And God's peace will keep your hearts and minds in Christ Jesus. That peace which God gives is so great that we cannot understand it.

     —Philippians 4:7 (ERV)

Grace and peace be multiplied to you in the knowledge of God and of Jesus our Lord.

     —2 Peter 1:2 (NKJV)

Presence of the HOLY SPIRIT

And the believers were filled with joy
and with the Holy Spirit.
>—*Acts 13:52 (NLT)*

Now may the God of hope fill you with
all joy and peace in believing, that you
may abound in hope by the power of
the Holy Spirit.
>—*Romans 15:13 (NKJV)*

Those who belong to Christ Jesus have
nailed the passions and desires of their
sinful nature to his cross and crucified
them there. Since we are living by the
Spirit, let us follow the Spirit's leading
in every part of our lives.
>—*Galatians 5:24–25 (NLT)*

God, your loyal followers are truly happy. They live in the light of your kindness.
       —*Psalm 89:15 (ERV)*

So if you sinful people know how to give good gifts to your children, how much more will your heavenly Father give the Holy Spirit to those who ask him.
       —*Luke 11:13 (NLT)*

The Lord answered, "I myself will go with you. I will lead you."
       —*Exodus 33:14 (ERV)*

You have made known to me the paths of life; you will fill me with joy in your presence.
       —*Acts 2:28 (NIV)*

Then Peter said to them, "Repent, and let every one of you be baptized in the name of Jesus Christ for the remission of sins; and you shall receive the gift of the Holy Spirit."
—*Acts 2:38 (NKJV)*

But when the Father sends the Advocate as my representative—that is, the Holy Spirit—he will teach you everything and will remind you of everything I have told you.
—*John 14:26 (NLT)*

Do not get drunk on wine, which leads to debauchery. Instead, be filled with the Spirit.
—*Ephesians 5:18 (NIV)*

Protection AND PROVISION

As for God, His way is perfect; the word of the LORD is proven; He is a shield to all who trust in Him.
> —*2 Samuel 22:31 (NKJV)*

The poor will eat and be satisfied. All who seek the LORD will praise him. Their hearts will rejoice with everlasting joy.
> —*Psalm 22:26 (NLT)*

Then you will have plenty to eat. You will be full. You will praise the name of the Lord your God. He has done wonderful things for you. My people will never again be ashamed.
> —*Joel 2:26 (ERV)*

And he said: "The LORD is my rock and my fortress and my deliverer; the God of my strength, in whom I will trust; my shield and the horn of my salvation, my stronghold and my refuge; my Savior, You save me from violence. I will call upon the LORD, who is worthy to be praised; so shall I be saved from my enemies."
—*2 Samuel 22:2–4 (NKJV)*

God, you are a hiding place for me. You protect me from my troubles. You surround me and protect me. So I sing about the way you saved me.
—*Psalm 32:7 (ERV)*

The angel of the LORD encamps all around those who fear Him, and delivers them.
—*Psalm 34:7 (NKJV)*

The cords of death entangled me; the torrents of destruction overwhelmed me. The cords of the grave coiled around me; the snares of death confronted me. In my distress I called to the LORD; I cried to my God for help. From his temple he heard my voice; my cry came before him, into his ears.

  —Psalm 18:4–6 (NIV)

He stores up sound wisdom for the upright; He is a shield to those who walk uprightly; He guards the paths of justice, and preserves the way of His saints.

  —Proverbs 2:7–8 (NKJV)

Give your burdens to the LORD, and he will take care of you. He will not permit the godly to slip and fall.

  —Psalm 55:22 (NLT)

May the LORD answer you in the day of trouble; may the name of the God of Jacob defend you; may He send you help from the sanctuary, and strengthen you out of Zion. . . . May He grant you according to your heart's desire, and fulfill all your purpose. We will rejoice in your salvation, and in the name of our God we will set up our banners! May the LORD fulfill all your petitions. Now I know that the LORD saves His anointed; He will answer him from His holy heaven with the saving strength of His right hand. Some trust in chariots, and some in horses; but we will remember the name of the LORD our God.

—*Psalm 20:1–2, 4–7 (NKJV)*

So bring your thank offerings to share with the other worshipers and come to be with God. You made promises to God Most High, so give him the things you promised. God says, "Call for me when you have troubles! I will help you. And then you can honor me."

—*Psalm 50:14–15 (ERV)*

The LORD is good, a refuge in times of trouble. He cares for those who trust in him.

—*Nahum 1:7 (NIV)*

When you have eaten and are satisfied, praise the LORD your God for the good land he has given you.

—*Deuteronomy 8:10 (NIV)*

Salvation

I tell you the truth. If a person hears what I say and believes in the One (God) who sent me, that person has life forever. That person will not be judged guilty. He has already left death and has entered into life.
> —*John 5:24 (ERV)*

The LORD is my strength and my song; he has given me victory. This is my God, and I will praise him—my father's God, and I will exalt him!
> —*Exodus 15:2 (NLT)*

If you confess with your mouth that Jesus is Lord and believe in your heart that God raised him from the dead, you will be saved.
> —*Romans 10:9 (NLT)*

I will greatly rejoice in the LORD, my soul shall be joyful in my God; for He has clothed me with the garments of salvation, He has covered me with the robe of righteousness, as a bridegroom decks himself with ornaments, and as a bride adorns herself with her jewels.

—Isaiah 61:10 (NKJV)

Why am I discouraged? Why is my heart so sad? I will put my hope in God! I will praise him again—my Savior and my God! Now I am deeply discouraged, but I will remember you—even from distant Mount Hermon, the source of the Jordan, from the land of Mount Mizar.

—Psalm 42:5–6 (NLT)

With joy you will drink deeply from the fountain of salvation!

—Isaiah 12:3 (NLT)

My sheep hear My voice, and I know them, and they follow Me. And I give them eternal life, and they shall never perish; neither shall anyone snatch them out of My hand.
—*John 10:27–28 (NKJV)*

Sing a new song to the Lord because he has done new and amazing things! His holy right arm brought him victory again. The Lord showed the nations his power to save. The Lord showed them his goodness.
—*Psalm 98:1–2 (ERV)*

At that time, people will say, "Here is our God! He is the One we have been waiting for. He has come to save us. We have been waiting for our Lord. So we will rejoice and be happy when the Lord saves us."
—*Isaiah 25:9 (ERV)*

So Christ was sacrificed once to take away the sins of many people; and he will appear a second time, not to bear sin, but to bring salvation to those who are waiting for him.

—Hebrews 9:28 (NIV)

My soul finds rest in God alone; my salvation comes from him. He alone is my rock and my salvation; he is my fortress, I will never be shaken.

—Psalm 62:1–2 (NIV)

But those who drink the water I give will never be thirsty again. It becomes a fresh, bubbling spring within them, giving them eternal life.

—John 4:14 (NLT)

Sing to the Lord, all the earth. Each day you must tell the good news about the Lord saving us.

—1 Chronicles 16:23 (ERV)

Being sorry like God wants makes a person change his heart and life. This leads a person to salvation, and we cannot be sorry for that. But the kind of sorrow the world has will bring death.
　　—*2 Corinthians 7:10 (ERV)*

Let all those who seek You rejoice and be glad in You; let such as love Your salvation say continually, "The LORD be magnified!"
　　—*Psalm 40:16 (NKJV)*

For that very reason I was shown mercy so that in me, the worst of sinners, Christ Jesus might display his unlimited patience as an example for those who would believe on him and receive eternal life.
　　—*1 Timothy 1:16 (NIV)*

D'S PROMISE

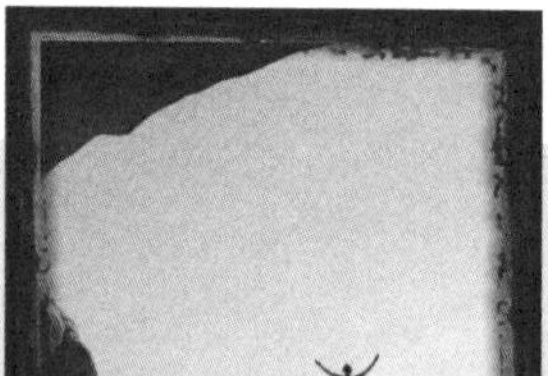

ROM

A SIMPLE WAY OF

Worshiping

And the priests attended to their services; the Levites also with istruments of the music of the LORD, which King David had made to praise the LORD, saying, "For His mercy endures forever," whenever David offered praise by their ministry. The priests sounded trumpets opposite them, while all Israel stood.

—2 Chronicles 7:6 (NKJV)

Praising GOD'S VERY NATURE

Have you never heard? Have you never understood? The LORD is the everlasting God, the Creator of all the earth. He never grows weak or weary. No one can measure the depths of his understanding. He gives power to the weak and strength to the powerless. Even youths will become weak and tired, and young men will fall in exhaustion. But those who trust in the LORD will find new strength. They will soar high on wings like eagles. They will run and not grow weary. They will walk and not faint.

—*Isaiah 40:28–31 (NLT)*

Ascribe to the LORD the glory due his name; worship the LORD in the splendor of his holiness.

—*Psalm 29:2 (NIV)*

Remember my special days of rest and honor my holy place. I am the Lord!

—*Leviticus 26:2 (ERV)*

For I know that the LORD is great, and our Lord is above all gods.

—*Psalm 135:5 (NKJV)*

I lift my eyes to you, O God, enthroned in heaven.

—*Psalm 123:1 (NLT)*

Celebrating GOD'S GOODNESS

Great is the LORD, and greatly to
be praised; and His greatness is
unsearchable. One generation shall
praise Your works to another, and shall
declare Your mighty acts. I will meditate
on the glorious splendor of Your
majesty, and on Your wondrous works.
Men shall speak of the might of Your
awesome acts, and I will declare Your
greatness. They shall utter the memory
of Your great goodness, and shall sing
of Your righteousness.

—Psalm 145:3–7 (NKJV)

But for you who fear my name, the Sun
of Righteousness will rise with healing
in his wings. And you will go free,
leaping with joy like calves let out to
pasture.

—Malachi 4:2 (NLT)

And now arise, O LORD God, and enter your resting place, along with the Ark, the symbol of your power. May your priests, O LORD God, be clothed with salvation; may your loyal servants rejoice in your goodness.
—*2 Chronicles 6:41 (NLT)*

What can I give to the Lord? The Lord gave me everything I have!
—*Psalm 116:12 (ERV)*

Worship the LORD with gladness; come before him with joyful songs. Know that the LORD is God. It is he who made us, and we are his; we are his people, the sheep of his pasture. Enter his gates with thanksgiving and his courts with praise; give thanks to him and praise his name. For the LORD is good and his love endures forever; his faithfulness continues through all generations.
—*Psalm 100:2–5 (NIV)*

Indeed it came to pass, when the trumpeters and singers were as one, to make one sound to be heard in praising and thanking the LORD, and when they lifted up their voice with the trumpets and cymbals and instruments of music, and praised the LORD, saying: "For He is good, for His mercy endures forever," that the house, the house of the LORD, was filled with a cloud.

—*2 Chronicles 5:13 (NKJV)*

I truly believe that I will see the Lord's goodness before I die.

—*Psalm 27:13 (ERV)*

Taste and see that the LORD is good; blessed is the man who takes refuge in him.

—*Psalm 34:8 (NIV)*

Worshiping TOGETHER

Come, let's bow down and worship him!
Let's praise the God who made us! He
is our God, and we are his people. We
are his sheep today—if we listen to his
voice.

—*Psalm 95:6–7 (ERV)*

Glorify the LORD with me; let us exalt
his name together.

—*Psalm 34:3 (NIV)*

Then David said to all the assembly,
"Now bless the LORD your God." So all
the assembly blessed the LORD God of
their fathers, and bowed their heads
and prostrated themselves before the
LORD and the king.

—*1 Chronicles 29:20 (NKJV)*

Exalting GOD

At the usual time for offering the evening sacrifice, Elijah the prophet walked up to the altar and prayed, "O LORD, God of Abraham, Isaac, and Jacob, prove today that you are God in Israel and that I am your servant. Prove that I have done all this at your command. O LORD, answer me! Answer me so these people will know that you, O LORD, are God and that you have brought them back to yourself."

—*1 Kings 18:36–37 (NLT)*

You must keep my Sabbath days of rest and show reverence for my sanctuary. I am the LORD.

—*Leviticus 26:2 (NLT)*

Know therefore that the LORD your God is God; he is the faithful God, keeping his covenant of love to a thousand generations of those who love him and keep his commands.
        —*Deuteronomy 7:9 (NIV)*

Know that the LORD, He is God; it is He who has made us, and not we ourselves; we are His people and the sheep of His pasture.
        —*Psalm 100:3 (NKJV)*

Be still, and know that I am God! I will be honored by every nation. I will be honored throughout the world.
        —*Psalm 46:10 (NLT)*

It is the LORD your God you must follow, and him you must revere. Keep his commands and obey him; serve him and hold fast to him.
        —*Deuteronomy 13:4 (NIV)*

So we should be thankful because we have a kingdom that cannot be shaken. We should be thankful and worship God in a way that will please him. We should worship him with respect and fear.

—*Hebrews 12:28 (ERV)*

I will give them hearts that recognize me as the LORD. They will be my people, and I will be their God, for they will return to me wholeheartedly.

—*Jeremiah 24:7 (NLT)*

# *God* IS WITH US

The Lord your God is with you. He is like a powerful soldier. He will save you. He will show how much he loves you. He will show you how happy he is with you. He will laugh and be happy about you.

—Zephaniah 3:17 (ERV)

The LORD is on my side; I will not fear. What can man do to me? The LORD is for me among those who help me; therefore I shall see my desire on those who hate me.

—Psalm 118:6–7 (NKJV)

The LORD replied, "I will personally go with you, Moses, and I will give you rest—everything will be fine for you."

—Exodus 33:14 (NLT)

Behold, I am with you and will keep you wherever you go, and will bring you back to this land; for I will not leave you until I have done what I have spoken to you.

—*Genesis 28:15 (NKJV)*

Don't be afraid, for I am with you. Don't be discouraged, for I am your God. I will strengthen you and help you. I will hold you up with my victorious right hand.

—*Isaiah 41:10 (NLT)*

God, your loyal followers are truly happy. They live in the light of your kindness. Your name always makes them happy. They praise your goodness. You are their amazing strength. Their power comes from you. Lord, you are our Protector. The Holy One of Israel is our King.

—*Psalm 89:15–18 (ERV)*

Surely you have granted him eternal blessings and made him glad with the joy of your presence.
                —Psalm 21:6 (NIV)

In my integrity you uphold me and set me in your presence forever. Praise be to the LORD, the God of Israel, from everlasting to everlasting. Amen and Amen.
                —Psalm 41:12–13 (NIV)

David also said to his son Solomon, "Be strong and brave and finish this work. Don't be afraid, because the Lord God, my God, is with you. He will help you until all the work is finished. He will not leave you. You will build the Lord's temple."
                —1 Chronicles 28:20 (ERV)

Then Haggai, the LORD'S messenger, spoke the LORD'S message to the people, saying, "I am with you, says the LORD."

—Haggai 1:13 (NKJV)

So go and make followers of all people in the world. Baptize them in the name of the Father and the Son and the Holy Spirit. Teach those people to obey everything that I have told you. You can be sure that I will be with you always. I will continue with you until the end of the world.

—Matthew 28:19–20 (ERV)

Jesus' EXAMPLE

Jesus answered, "It is written in the Scriptures: 'You must worship the Lord your God. Serve only him!'"
—*Luke 4:8 (ERV)*

After Jesus said these things he looked toward heaven. Jesus prayed, "Father, the time has come. Give glory to your Son so that the Son can give glory to you. You gave the Son power over all people so that the Son could give eternal life to all those people you have given to him. And this is eternal life: that people can know you, the only true God, and that people can know Jesus Christ, the One you sent."
—*John 17:1–3 (ERV)*

Yet a time is coming and has now come when the true worshipers will worship the Father in spirit and truth, for they are the kind of worshipers the Father seeks.

　　　—John 4:23 (NIV)

D’S PROMIS

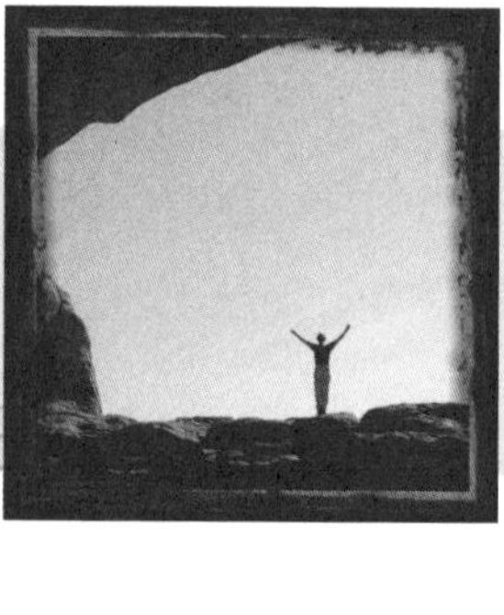

RON

EXAMPLES OF

Worship

*Give thanks to the Lord,
for he is good! His faithful
love endures forever.*

—Psalm 136:1 (NLT)

Angels

And suddenly there was with the angel a multitude of the heavenly host praising God and saying: "Glory to God in the highest, and on earth peace, goodwill toward men!"
> —*Luke 2:13–14 (NKJV)*

Then I looked again, and I heard the voices of thousands and millions of angels around the throne and of the living beings and the elders. And they sang in a mighty chorus: "Worthy is the Lamb who was slaughtered—to receive power and riches and wisdom and strength and honor and glory and blessing."
> —*Revelation 5:11–12 (NLT)*

The elders and the four living things
were there. All the angels were standing
around them and the throne. The
angels bowed down on their faces
before the throne and worshiped
God. They said, "Amen! Praise, glory,
wisdom, thanks, honor, power, and
strength belong to our God forever and
ever. Amen!"
        —*Revelation 7:11–12 (ERV)*

Praise the LORD, you his angels, you
mighty ones who do his bidding, who
obey his word. Praise the LORD, all his
heavenly hosts, you his servants who
do his will.
        —*Psalm 103:20–21 (NIV)*

And when God brings his firstborn Son
into the world, he says, "Let all God's
angels worship the Son."
        —*Hebrews 1:6 (ERV)*

Praise the LORD! Praise the LORD from the heavens; praise Him in the heights! Praise Him, all His angels; praise Him, all His hosts!
    —*Psalm 148:1–2 (NKJV)*

Daniel

That night the secret was revealed to Daniel in a vision. Then Daniel praised the God of heaven. He said, "Praise the name of God forever and ever, for he has all wisdom and power. He controls the course of world events; he removes kings and sets up other kings. He gives wisdom to the wise and knowledge to the scholars. He reveals deep and mysterious things and knows what lies hidden in darkness, though he is surrounded by light. I thank and praise you, God of my ancestors, for you have given me wisdom and strength. You have told me what we asked of you and revealed to us what the king demanded."

—Daniel 2:19–23 (NLT)

David

Give thanks to the LORD, for he is
good.
   His love endures forever.
Give thanks to the God of gods.
   His love endures forever.
Give thanks to the Lord of lords:
   His love endures forever.
To him who alone does great wonders,
   His love endures forever.
Who by his understanding made the
heavens,
   His love endures forever.
Who spread out the earth upon the
waters,
   His love endures forever.
Who made the great lights—
   His love endures forever.
The sun to govern the day,
   His love endures forever.

The moon and stars to govern the night;
His love endures forever.
To the One who remembered us in our low estate
His love endures forever.
And freed us from our enemies,
His love endures forever.
And who gives food to every creature.
His love endures forever.
Give thanks to the God of heaven.
His love endures forever.
—*Psalm 136:1–9, 23–26 (NIV)*

Deborah AND BARAK

On the day that the people of Israel
defeated Sisera, Deborah and Barak
son of Abinoam sang this song:

The men of Israel prepared for battle.
They volunteered to go to war! Bless the
Lord!

Listen, kings. Pay attention, rulers. I
will sing. I myself will sing to the Lord. I
will make music to the Lord, to the God
of the people of Israel.

Lord, in the past you came from Seir.
You marched from the land of Edom.
You marched and the earth shook. The
skies rained. The clouds dropped water.
The mountains shook before the Lord,
the God of Mount Sinai, before the
Lord, the God of Israel!

In the days of Shamgar son of Anath,
and in the days of Jael, the main roads

were empty. Caravans and travelers traveled on the back roads.

There were no soldiers. There were no soldiers in Israel until you came, Deborah, until you came to be a mother to Israel.

God chose new leaders to fight at the city gates. No one could find a shield or a spear among the 40,000 soldiers of Israel.

My heart is with the commanders of Israel who volunteered to go to war! Bless the Lord!

Pay attention you people riding on white donkeys, sitting on saddle blankets, and walking along the road! At the watering holes for the animals, we hear the music of cymbals. People sing about the victories of the Lord, the victories of his soldiers in Israel when the Lord's people fought at the city gates and won!

Wake up, wake up, Deborah! Wake up, wake up, sing the song! Get up, Barak! Go capture your enemies, son of Abinoam! . . .

May all your enemies die like this, Lord! And may all the people who love you be strong like the rising sun!

So there was peace in the land for 40 years.

—*Judges 5:1–12, 31 (ERV)*

Hannah

Then Hannah prayed and said: "My heart rejoices in the LORD; in the LORD my horn is lifted high. My mouth boasts over my enemies, for I delight in your deliverance. There is no one holy like the LORD; there is no one besides you; there is no Rock like our God. . . . The LORD sends poverty and wealth; he humbles and he exalts. He raises the poor from the dust and lifts the needy from the ash heap; he seats them with princes and has them inherit a throne of honor. For the foundations of the earth are the LORD's; upon them he has set the world. He will guard the feet of his saints, but the wicked will be silenced in darkness. It is not by strength that one prevails."

—1 Samuel 2:1–2, 7–9 (NIV)

Mary

And Mary said: "My soul glorifies the Lord and my spirit rejoices in God my Savior, for he has been mindful of the humble state of his servant. From now on all generations will call me blessed, for the Mighty One has done great things for me—holy is his name. His mercy extends to those who fear him, from generation to generation. He has performed mighty deeds with his arm; he has scattered those who are proud in their inmost thoughts. He has brought down rulers from their thrones but has lifted up the humble. He has filled the hungry with good things but has sent the rich away empty. He has helped his servant Israel, remembering to be merciful to Abraham and his descendants forever, even as he said to our fathers."

—_Luke 1:46–55 (NIV)_

Moses

Then Moses and the people of Israel began singing this song to the Lord:

"I will sing to the Lord! He has done great things. He threw horse and rider into the sea. The Lord is my strength. He saves me, and I sing songs of praise to him. The Lord is my God, and I praise him. The Lord is the God of my ancestors, and I honor him. The Lord is a great soldier. The Lord is his name. He threw Pharaoh's chariots and soldiers into the sea. Pharaoh's very best soldiers drowned in the Red Sea. The deep water covered them. And they sank to the bottom like rocks.

"Your right arm is amazingly strong. Lord, your right arm shattered the enemy.

"Are there any gods like the Lord? No! There are no gods like you—You are wonderfully holy! You are amazingly powerful! You do great miracles! You could raise your right hand and destroy the world! But with your kindness you lead the people you saved. And with your strength you lead them to your holy and pleasant land. Lord, you will lead your people to your mountain. You will let them live near the place you prepared for your throne. Master, you will build your temple! The Lord will rule forever and ever!"

—*Exodus 15:1–6, 11–13, 17–18 (ERV)*

Simeon

Now there was a man in Jerusalem called Simeon, who was righteous and devout. He was waiting for the consolation of Israel, and the Holy Spirit was upon him. It had been revealed to him by the Holy Spirit that he would not die before he had seen the Lord's Christ. Moved by the Spirit, he went into the temple courts. When the parents brought in the child Jesus to do for him what the custom of the Law required, Simeon took him in his arms and praised God, saying: "Sovereign Lord, as you have promised, you now dismiss your servant in peace. For my eyes have seen your salvation, which you have prepared in the sight of all people, a light for revelation to the Gentiles and for glory to your people Israel."

—*Luke 2:25–32 (NIV)*

Solomon

"Praise the LORD, the God of Israel, who has kept the promise he made to my father, David. For he told my father, 'From the day I brought my people out of the land of Egypt, I have never chosen a city among any of the tribes of Israel as the place where a Temple should be built to honor my name. Nor have I chosen a king to lead my people Israel. But now I have chosen Jerusalem as the place for my name to be honored, and I have chosen David to be king over my people Israel.'"

Then Solomon said, "My father, David, wanted to build this Temple to honor the name of the LORD, the God of Israel. But the LORD told him, 'You wanted to build the Temple to honor my name. Your intention is good, but you are not the one to do it. One of your own sons will build the Temple to honor me.'

"And now the LORD has fulfilled the promise he made, for I have become king in my father's place, and now I sit on the throne of Israel, just as the LORD promised. I have built this Temple to honor the name of the LORD, the God of Israel. There I have placed the Ark, which contains the covenant that the LORD made with the people of Israel."

—*2 Chronicles 6:4–11 (NLT)*

Zechariah

Then his father, Zechariah, was filled with the Holy Spirit and gave this prophecy:

"Praise the Lord, the God of Israel, because he has visited and redeemed his people. He has sent us a mighty Savior from the royal line of his servant David, just as he promised through his holy prophets long ago. Now we will be saved from our enemies and from all who hate us. He has been merciful to our ancestors by remembering his sacred covenant—the covenant he swore with an oath to our ancestor Abraham. We have been rescued from our enemies so we can serve God without fear, in holiness and righteousness for as long as we live.

"And you, my little son, will be called the prophet of the Most High, because you will prepare the way for the Lord. You will tell his people how to find salvation through forgiveness of their sins. Because of God's tender mercy, the morning light from heaven is about to break upon us, to give light to those who sit in darkness and in the shadow of death, and to guide us to the path of peace."

—*Luke 1:67–79 (NLT)*